DEDICATION

This is the work of two young Learners, Mawuena Akafia (9 years) and Senyefia Kpedor (8years). This book is dedicated to the families of the first six Learners of Pioneers International Academy. In January 2016, six learners, Mawuena Akafia, Senyefia Kpedor, Senam Kpedor, Sedinam Kpedor, Elinam Afeku, Elikem Afeku and their families, joined us in our journey to develop Africa's children capacity to make an impact in the world. Since then our numbers have increased and many families have joined our team. It is our hope and determination that these pioneering students and all those who have joined or will join us subsequently, will see the long-term results of their belief and investment in our school. To the parents of Mawuena and Senyefia, we hope that your children have made you proud by their work.

D1378952

CONTENT

ACKNOWLEDGMENTS

We give great thanks to the teachers of Pioneers for working with Mawuena and Senyefia in their research leading to the writing of this book. We also acknowledge the various Ghanaians who are presented in this book for their contribution to the country. To the families of the Ghanaians presented here who have since departed from our world, we are grateful that they made information readily available for our students to learn and write about their exploits. To our friends in Ghana and Abroad, who helped edit this book and support its publication, God richly bless you. It is our hope that this will be the beginning of many works by the Learners of Pioneers International Academy.

General Information & Important Facts

1. Ghana means "Warrior King" in the Mande language.

2. Ghana was named after the ancient Ghana Empire, which existed from the 6th to the 13th Century.

3. Ghana used to be called the Gold Coast. The Portuguese who colonized Ghana found a lot of gold in the 15th century, particularly near the River Ankobra. We think Ghana was called Gold Coast because of the gold there. The location of modern day Ghana is different from the Ancient Empire of Ghana. The name Ghana was adopted on attaining independence from the United Kingdom in 1957.

4. The official residence and office of the president of Ghana is the Flagstaff House, also called the Golden Jubilee House. Some presidents work in the flagstaff house and continue to live in their private residences. The seat of government used to be at the Osu Castle.

Golden Jubilee House

Osu Castle

5. The currency in Ghana is Cedis and Pesewas. Before independence, Ghana used West African pounds, shillings and pence. Ghana started using Cedis and pesewas on July 19ʰ, 1965. (One hundred pesewas make one cedi)

6. Ghana is the world's second largest producer of cocoa. A Ghanaian agriculturist, Tetteh Quarshie, introduced cocoa to Ghana in 1876 on his return from the Island of Fernando Po (Bioko) in modern day Equatorial Guinea. Cocoa is used to make body lotions, beverages, toffees, chocolates and many more. You absolutely should taste Ghana's Golden Tree Chocolate. It is made from the best cocoa, in our opinion.

Cocoa fruit, Cocoa butter and Golden Tree Chocolate.

7. Lake Volta, located in the Volta Region, is the third largest lake in the world. It is also the largest man-made lake in the world. It is the source of Ghana's main hydroelectric power supply through the Akosombo Dam. One of the problems we have, however, is when it does not rain as much as is needed, Volta Lake drops in volume and further affects our supply of water to the Akosombo Dam. This leads to a rationing of electricity supply to many homes in Ghana. This rationing of electricity is called 'Dumsor'. It means power goes 'off and on.' Do you know that Dumsor can now be found on Wikipedia?

Volta lake showing Akosombo dam

8. The Greenwich Meridian passes through Ghana through a city called Tema. This is why Ghana is on Greenwich Meridian Time. (GMT).

9. The country's capital, Accra, is located close to longitude $0°$ and latitude $0°$. This makes Ghana the closest country to the center of the world.

10. There are over 100 ethnic groups in Ghana. Each group has a distinct culture, language, and history. Some of these ethnic groups are the Akans, the Ewes, the Gas, and the Guans.

History

11. Ghana gained independence from the British on 6ᵗʰ March, 1957. Even though several people and organizations worked hard for Ghana's independence, there were a group of six champions called 'The Big Six' who were the leaders for independence. One of them, Dr. Kwame Nkrumah, subsequently became the first president of Ghana after independence from the British. Every sixth of March people from all walks of life, including students, celebrate Ghana's Independence Day. Schools always hold a march at the Independence Square in Accra. This is very close to the Polo Grounds where Ghana's independence was declared in 1957.

Independence Square

12. Since Ghana's independence, there have been four Republics. A new Republic starts each time a new constitution is made to govern the people. The reason for the many republics is that there have been several *coup d'états* in Ghana where governments have been overthrown by the military. Ghana has, however, not had a coup since 1981 and has had its current constitution since 1992.

13. The first president of the First Republic of Ghana was Dr. Kwame Nkrumah. He was born on 21 September, 1909 and died on 27 April, 1972.

Kwame Nkrumah

14. The first president of the fourth republic of Ghana was Jerry John Rawlings. President Rawlings was first a military ruler before, under his leadership, the country once again became a democracy in 1992. The Fourth Republic has, so far, had four presidents, all who have the name John. On 7 January of 2017, the fifth president of the Fourth Republic was sworn in. His name was not John. He is Nana Addo Dankwa Akufo-Addo.

15. The second president of the fourth republic was John Agyekum Kuffour.

16.The third president of the fourth republic was John Atta Mills. He was a law professor for many years before becoming a politician.

17.The fourth president of the was John Dramani Mahama. He was the vice president of Ghana when President John Attah Mills was the president.

18. The fifth president of the Forth Republic is Nana Addo Dankwa Akufo Addo. Three of "the Big Six" - the people who faught for Ghana's independence were his relatives; J. B Danquah (grand uncle), William Ofori-Atta (uncle) and Edward Akufo- Addo- his father.

Country Symbols

19. The colours of Ghana's flag are red, yellow, and green with a black star in the middle. The red represents the people who died during the struggle for independence. The yellow represents the country's minerals and natural resources. The green represents Ghana's rich forest, and the black star represents the unity and freedom of the people of Africa.

20. Ghana's Coat of Arms is made up of a sword on the upper left side. On the upper right side is Osu Castle, the former seat of government. There is a cocoa tree on the lower left and a gold mine the lower right. In the middle of the shield is a golden lion. Do you want to know what the symbols represent? Well, that is your assignment from us. Make sure you research it.

21. The Adinkra Symbols are used by the Ashanti people to represent values and beliefs of their culture.

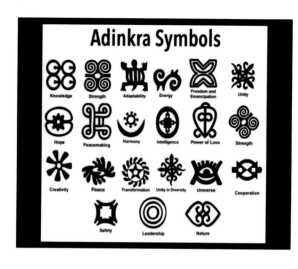

22. The currency symbol for the Ghanaian cedi is a small "c" with a line slashed through it.

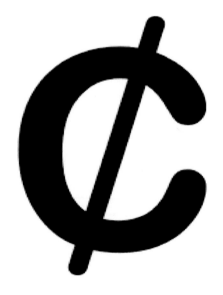

Geography & Weather

23. Ghana is in West Africa.

The country north of Ghana is Burkina Faso. The country east of Ghana is Togo. The country west of Ghana is Ivory Coast. The Gulf of Guinea is south of Ghana. All the countries around Ghana speak French even though Ghanaians speak English. Ghana is bordered on the south by the Atlantic Ocean.

24. Ghana is divided into ten regions, namely: Greater Accra, Central, Volta, Eastern, Western, Ashanti, Brong-Ahafo, Northern, Upper West, and Upper East.

25. Mountain Afadjato is the tallest mountain in Ghana. It is 885 metres, or 2,904 feet tall. It is in the Volta Region of Ghana. Afadja is the actual name of the mountain and 'to' means mountain in the Ewe Language. So, whenever people say "Mountain Afadjato" they are actually saying "Mountain Afadja Mountain."

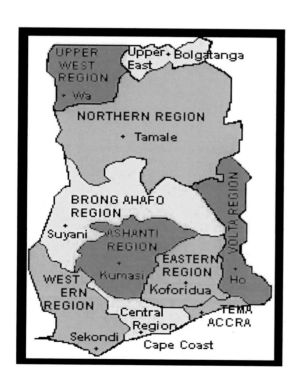

18

26. Ghana has a warm climate. This is because it is a little higher than the equator, and so it receives a lot of sunlight. Ghana is located in the Tropical Zone.

27. There are two seasons in Ghana; the dry season and the wet season. The rainy season starts from March to November in the northern part of Ghana and from April to mid-November in the southern part of Ghana.

28. The Harmattan is a dry, dusty wind that blows in Ghana during the dry season, from late December to mid-February. It blows from the northern part of Africa, or the Sahara Desert, and it is called the Northeast Trade Wind.

Famous People Born in Ghana

29. Okomfo Anokye was a spiritual priest who performed many wonders, like placing a sword in the ground which could never be taken out. His greatest wonder was bringing down a golden stool from the sky that represents the soul and strength of the Ashanti people.

30. Yaa Asantewaa was the queen mother of Ejisu, a town in the Ashanti region. When the British wanted to fight the Ashantis and take the Golden Stool, Yaa Asantewaa led her people to war. She is one of the bravest women in Ghana's history.

31. Theodosia Okoh is the person who designed Ghana's flag. She was born on 13 June, 1922 and she died on 19 April, 2015.

32. Kofi Atta Annan (born 8 April, 1938) is a Ghanaian diplomat who served as the seventh Secretary-General of the United Nations from January 1997 to December 2006.

33. Ama Ata Aidoo, née Christina Ama Aidoo, is a Ghanaian author, poet, playwright and academic, who was born on 23 March, 1942 in a town called Saltpond, in the Central Region. Some of her books include *Anowa* and *No Sweetness Here*. She was once Ghana's Minister of Education.

34. Kofi Ghanaba (Guy Warren) was a Ghanaian musician who invented Afro-jazz. Afro-jazz is jazz music that has been mixed with African beats and rhythms. His stage name was Kofi Ghanaba (Ghanaba means a child of Ghana). He was born on 4 May, 1923 and died on 22 December, 2008.

35. Abedi Ayew is a retired Ghanaian footballer who was the captain of Ghana's national team, the Blackstars. He was so good in football, that people named him after Pele of Brazil (one of the best footballers in the world) and gave him the nickname "Abedi Pele". Three of Abedi's children Ibrahim Ayew, Dede Ayew and Jordan Ayew also play for the Ghana Blackstars.

36. Esther Ocloo was an industrialist, an entrepreneur and one of the founders of Women's World Banking, a global microfinance organisation that provides financial and developmental services to entrepreneurs to help them expand their businesses. She established Nukulenu Industries, a pioneer in food processing in Ghana. For her work in helping to reduce poverty, Esther Ocloo was the first woman recipient of the global Hunger Project Award in 2000. She was born in 1919 and died in 2002.

37. Komla Dumor was a talented Ghanaian journalist who won the Ghanaian Journalist of the Year Award in 2003. He started his career at a Ghanaian radio station called Joy FM and subsequently worked for the British Broadcasting Corporation (BBC) in radio and television. He was known for telling true and balanced stories about Africa. He also mentored several journalists and young people to be the best in whatever they did. He was born on 3 October, 1972 and died on 18 January, 2014.

Culture

Food

38. There are different types of dishes unique to the different ethnic groups in Ghana. Some of them are Fufu (pounded plantain & cassava) with soup, banku with okro soup, akple, and "Red", (a dish made from ripe plantain and red-eyed beans).

Clothing

39. There are also different types of clothing worn by the different ethnic groups. Some of them are Kente, a brightly coloured woven cloth that originates from the Ashanti and Volta regions of Ghana.

40. The smock is a plaid shirt with both male and female versions and originates from the Northern Region.

Dances

41. Ghana has many different traditional dances. For example, Agbadza is a war dance of the Ewe people of Ghana. The Ewe people in Benin and Togo also use this dance. It involves spreading your arms wide apart and moving your waist back and forth to the rhythm.

Agbadza dance

42. Boboobo is a dance that originated from Kpando in the Volta Region of Ghana. It is also called Agbeyeye, which means New Life, or Akpese which means Music of Joy. Other dances include Adowa from the Ashanti region, kpanlogo from the Greater Accra region and Bambaya from the northern region.

Bambaya Dance

Festivals

43. All over Ghana, festivals are celebrated by the various ethnic groups for different reasons. Some celebrate festivals to honour their ancestors and others celebrate new harvests on their farms.

44. The Aboakyir is a bushbuck hunting festival is celebrated by the Efutu people of Winneba in the Central Region. The people hunt for deer to sacrifice to one of their gods called "Penkye Otu". They celebrate the festival in May.

Tourism

45. There are many slave castles used by the Europeans when they first came here. They used the castles to keep slaves and fight the enemies. The Cape Coast Castle and the Elmina Castles, both in the Central Region, are two of about forty slave castles in Ghana.

Cape Coast Castle

46. NZULEZU (The Town on a River): The village of **Nzulezo** (or Nzulezu) is located in the Western Region of Ghana. It made up of many homes, a couple of churches, some schools and community centres, all built on water. When the children reach a higher grade in school they travel by canoes to go to school in a nearby town.

47. Kakum National Park is a tropical rainforest located in the Central Region of Ghana. There is a canopy walkway which is 350 metres (1,150 feet) long and it enables you to see the forest from the tree tops The Kakum Forest has a lot of wildlife like monkeys, elephants, antelopes and about 250 species of birds.

48. Mole National Park is Ghana's largest wildlife refuge, and is located in the Northern Region. It has over 300 species of birds and mammals such as elephants, antelopes, warthogs, baboons, lions and leopards. Birds include martial eagles, the white-headed and palm-nut vultures, herons, egrets, the Abyssinian roller and the red-throated bee-eater. You have to visit the Mole national park if you ever come to Ghana.

Elephants at Mole national park

49. The Kwame Nkrumah Mausoleum and Memorial Park is found in Accra. The bodies of Ghana's first president, Kwame Nkrumah, and his wife are buried inside the mausoleum. The museum, which is also in the park, has some belongings and pictures of Kwame Nkrumah that show his life history. Many people go to the mausoleum to learn more about Kwame Nkrumah.

50. The Bobiri Forest Reserve and Butterfly Sanctuary is the only butterfly sanctuary in West Africa. It has about 400 species of butterflies. It is in the village of Kubease, about 30 kilometres (19 mi) from one of Ghana's major cities, Kumasi. It was created in 1931 and has an area of 54.65 km^2 (21.10 sq. mi).

51. Ghana's coast is made up of a long stretch of beaches for relaxation and recreational purposes. Some of these are Labadi Beach in Accra (Greater Accra Region) and Busua beach in Takoradi (Western Region). There are also a lot of beautiful waterfalls spread throughout the country. Most of these falls are seasonal and start at the end of the main rainy season. The Wli Falls is the highest waterfall in Ghana and West Africa and is located in the Volta Region. It is 80 metres high.

Wli waterfall, krokrobite beach and white sands beach

THE END

About the Authors:

Mawuena Akafia is 9years old and Year 5 student at Pioneers International Academy. His favourite subjects are Science and Math. He loves reading and always picks up a book in his free time. He loves Minecraft and building with his LEGO. He says both activities increase his creativity and imagination. He wants to be an Electrical Engineer and a Ninja.

Senyefia Kpedor is 8 years old and a Year 4 student at Pioneers International Academy. His favourite subject is Science and he loves to experiment and build things out of nothing. He also likes his literacy class because it helps him speak properly. In his free time, he likes to code on the computer and ride his bike around the neighborhood. He wants to be a Computer Engineer.

Mawuena Akafia and Senyefia kpedor as cast of *Ananse and the Gum Statute*, a drama performance in December 2016

Ms. Jennifer Aye Addo is a science enthusiast who loves to pass on her love for science to her students. She likes to teach and interact with students because of their excitement and joy over learning new things; it's contagious. Ms. Jennifer is a graduate from University of Maryland in Molecular Genetics. She started the book project with Mawuena and Senyefia and in April 2017 she started medical school in Ghana. She wants to specialize in anesthesiology.

Pioneers provides quality affordable international Early Childhood, Primary and High School education across Africa, starting with Ghana. Using the Cambridge International curriculum, with emphasis on leadership, innovation and community engagement, Pioneers develop our Learners to be more than just knowledgeable. We aim to produce life-long learners, who are inquirers, thinkers, risk takers, yet principled, balanced and passionate about contributing to improving the world. We focus on STEM (Science, Technology, Engineering and Math) to develop learners who build their curiosity, skills and interest in these fields. We use Lego Education resources to enable our learners find fun and interesting ways to collaborate and develop solutions to some of the pressing issues of our time. Our long-term goal is to makes our schools available in all places of need across Africa starting with Ghana.

Pioneers International Academy
Dawhenya, Ghana
+233 544 068256; +233 560 822982; +233-208661373
info@pioneers-edu.com; www.pioneers-edu.com

Made in the USA
Lexington, KY
23 June 2018